GREAT EXIT PROJECTS ON THE EASTERN HEMISPHERE

GREAT EXIT PROJECTS ON THE

EASTERN
HEMISPHERE

Bridey Heing

rosen publishing's
rosen
central®

New York

Published in 2020 by The Rosen Publishing Group, Inc.
29 East 21st Street, New York, NY 10010

First Edition

Library of Congress Cataloging-in-Publication Data

Names: Heing, Bridey, author.
Title: Great exit projects on the Eastern hemisphere / Bridey Heing.
Description: First edition. | New York, NY : The Rosen Publishing Group, Inc., 2020. | Series: Great social studies exit projects | Includes bibliographical references and index.
Identifiers: LCCN 2018012922| ISBN 9781499440409 (library bound) | ISBN 9781499440393 (pbk.)
Subjects: LCSH: Eastern hemisphere—Study and teaching. | Civilization, Oriental—Study and teaching.
Classification: LCC D891 .H45 2019 | DDC 909/.09811—dc23
LC record available at https://lccn.loc.gov/2018012922

Manufactured in the United States of America

CONTENTS

We have many ways of understanding the regions of our world. By dividing the many countries and continents into two equal halves, or hemispheres, we can study the relationship between the many parts of the earth—from the peoples who populate it to the history that shaped the regions to the climates that exist within countries. Studying an entire hemisphere opens up possibilities to make connections about the way our world is connected, and it provides an opportunity to find a deeper understanding about those connections.

The Eastern Hemisphere begins in the United Kingdom at the Prime Meridian and stretches east to include Australia and other Oceania nations. Europe, Asia, and Africa are all part of the Eastern Hemisphere, making it home to a wide range of cultures and peoples. In fact, 82 percent of all people live in the Eastern Hemisphere, while 18 percent live in the Western Hemisphere.

The diversity of the Eastern Hemisphere has fueled a complex history that has shaped the trajectory of humanity. Some of the earliest civilizations on earth began in the Eastern Hemisphere, and historic trade routes like the Silk Road connected these cultures in ways that changed our world forever. Interaction between cultures gave rise to alliances and rivalries between civilizations, while merchants who traveled across the hemisphere brought with them new religions, goods, and knowledge.

It was also in the Eastern Hemisphere that the consolidation of power that would shape the entire world came about, with great power centers from which authority radiated. Empires like the Chinese, Persians, Ottomans, and Egyptians rose, fell, and

The Eastern Hemisphere, shown here, includes the majority of the world's population and multiple continents. It stretches from Western Europe to Australia.

conquered the eastern world for centuries. But in the 1400s European empires began explorations that would take them to the farthest reaches of the hemisphere, where colonization took place. The practice of colonization, by which a state takes control of a region and its resources, became the defining moment in the history of much of the Eastern Hemisphere, while in Europe the age of empire shaped relationships between powerful ruling families.

But that changed in the twentieth century, when two World Wars and a wave of independence movements against colonial rule changed the way the Eastern Hemisphere was governed. Along with issues related to climate change, ongoing conflict, and economic uncertainty, the ramifications of colonization and the collapse of empire are still being worked through by many states within the Eastern Hemisphere.

This collection of example projects, which can be used as models for students who are crafting their own exit projects, will take readers from the ancient world to modern cities, tracing the history of the Eastern Hemisphere. The projects in this book model ways to question, think about, and shape projects that explore some of history's defining moments and movements, as well as how to think about topics in relation to multiple countries within the same region.

CHAPTER ONE

THE BEGINNINGS OF CIVILIZATION

Across the Eastern Hemisphere, you can find ruins and artifacts from ancient civilizations. Cities like Alexandria, Rome, and Baghdad—along with countries like Russia, China, Japan, Ethiopia, and France—have complex histories

The Eastern Hemisphere is home to some of the oldest ruins in the world, which have taught us a great deal about early civilizations.

that began millennia ago. Some of the world's first major cities, which also served as hubs for trade and government, emerged in Asia and the Mediterranean. These city-states made contact with one another along complex trade routes that crossed land and sea, bringing together peoples from Britain to Oceania. From these early civilizations empires grew, religions emerged, and traditions were established that would eventually shape the world we know today.

QUESTION 1 WHAT LED TO THE RISE OF THE FIRST CIVILIZATIONS IN THE EASTERN HEMISPHERE?

Some of the first complex civilizations on earth emerged in the Eastern Hemisphere, ranging from African empires to Asian city-states. The first known complex civilization emerged in modern-day Iraq. Sumer in Mesopotamia emerged around 4000 BCE, and it was where early forms of written language— or cuneiform—are believed to have originated around 3000 BCE. Other civilizations and city-states emerged soon after, including those in modern Lebanon, China, India, and along the Mediterranean. These civilizations took on many forms but emerged for similar reasons.

One of the most significant changes in the history of mankind was the shift toward agriculture over foraging as a mode of food production. This change allowed communities to settle rather than travel as nomads, which in turn made it possible for specialties to be taken up, such as woodworking or carpentry. From these early groups, large civilizations and empires developed, they were ruled over most often by kings or other absolute rulers. Peoples came together for a variety of reasons, most often related to a shared history or culture, which gave rise to our understanding of national identity.

Geography often played a large part in the development of cities and other urban-like spaces, with access to resources playing an important role in establishing trade or military power. The spread of technology, particularly between the Bronze and Iron Ages, was also an important driver for the growth and spread of civilizations; it allowed peoples to develop new weapons and trade goods, which strengthened their governance.

ANCIENT EUROPE

The study of civilization in the ancient world is focused primarily on the Mediterranean, the Middle East, and Asia. But central and western Europe were also undergoing important shifts that laid the foundation for today's understanding of these areas. The Bronze Age was a period of tribal rule in much of Europe, with isolated groups ruling parts of Germany and France among other modern states. In modern Britain, invasion and immigration defined a changing island. During the Iron Age, Celtic, Gallic, and Germanic tribes dominated the region until around 1 CE, when Rome expanded its empire to include much of Europe.

PROJECT 1
THE CRADLE OF CIVILIZATION

Research Mesopotamia and its placement among other contemporary civilizations, then create a map that shows the geography of the ancient world.

Using modern resources to map the ancient world can help us understand how technology developed, why trade evolved as it did, and how some cities flourished.

- Using resources such as reputable online sources or your school library, gather information about Mesopotamia. This can include its history, major city-states within the area, and forms of government.
- Using your information about the time frame during which Mesopotamia flourished, gather information about other civilizations that existed at the same time. To do so, research regions that were developing in ancient times, such as China, Eurasia, the Levant, the Mediterranean, North Africa, and the Indian subcontinent.

- Find a map that shows the layout of the ancient world, particularly focused on Mesopotamia. Create a list of the civilizations you want to map in your notebook, making note of the dates they existed. Create your map using either a template or freehand drawing.
- Starting with Mesopotamia, label the map with what civilizations you found, including the time frame during which they existed. You can mark the area the civilization existed in by shading it in or labeling its capital. Make a note of any civilizations with multiple capitals and state on your map what span of years your map represents.
- Your map should show the makeup of the ancient world, with a diverse range of civilizations that span the Eastern Hemisphere.

QUESTION 2 HOW DID EARLY CIVILIZATIONS DIFFER FROM ONE ANOTHER?

Although ancient civilizations emerged for similar reasons, they differed widely in culture, politics, and resources. Different civilizations had access to different tools, knowledge, and levels of prosperity, all of which played a role in their development. For example, civilizations in the Indian subcontinent consistently developed along waterways that made it possible and critical that they develop technology to enable sea trade, while Mesopotamian civilizations emerged in landlocked areas where farming and irrigation methods were more important.

But some things emerged at similar times and for similar reasons, such as religious or artistic practices. This is in part due to the role trade played in connecting civilizations. Knowledge and information could be spread across the ancient world, and with it techniques that influenced the development of culture, clothing, crafts, cooking, and other aspects of life in major urban centers. In many cases, though, skills or knowledge developed independently within multiple regions, indicating a universal value for mankind.

PROJECT 2
DEVELOPING TOOLS OF LANGUAGE

Create a presentation that compares and contrasts forms of written language, including the development of these languages and how they spread.

- Using the internet or your school library, research early forms of writing.This can include proto-writing in places like China, Mesopotamia, the Indian subcontinent, and northern Africa.
- For your own use, create a timeline of how written language developed in the areas you will focus on. How did writing evolve through the Bronze and Iron Ages? How were the forms of writing different? Find or make your own illustrations of early writing to use as examples.
- What was writing used for in these civilizations? Was it reserved for certain classes or was access to writing spread wide in society? How did this impact its development?
- Using a free online resource or a diagram, put your information into presentation form. This could be a

Presenting to the class can be scary, but it is a chance for you to share things you found interesting about your research and to inform others in an engaging way.

timeline that shows when and where different forms of writing emerged or a graphic that includes information and illustrations on how writing evolved in different parts of the ancient world.

- Your presentation should include examples of ancient writing, discussion of how each form differed from writing styles that came before it and that were used in different parts of the world, and what writing meant to the peoples who used it.

CHAPTER TWO

TRADE IN THE ANCIENT WORLD

Trade was one of the most important facets of the ancient world. It built strong economies, facilitated exchanges of culture and information, and helped motivate the exploration of our world. Trade was also a source of innovation; new technology made it possible for sailors to navigate the seas

Trade routes, like the Silk Road, were key to the development of civilizations and cities, which became leading hubs of technology and culture.

and for routes to be traversed by land. Along trade routes cities and caravansarai, or small cities that developed specifically to support traders and merchants, emerged where people and merchants from around the ancient world could interact. Trade also made it possible for civilizations and peoples to maintain peace—economic strength and resource access meant creating alliances, allowing entire regions to thrive.

QUESTION 3 HOW DID TRADE ROUTES DEVELOP IN THE ANCIENT WORLD?

Trade routes in the ancient world connected civilizations and pushed culture forward, and routes existed between civilizations that emerged in distant parts of the world. Routes by land, such as the Silk Road and the Amber Road, stretched from China to the Mediterranean, while sea routes such as the Spice Route connected Africa, Europe, and East Asia through the Indian subcontinent. Civilizations became wealthy from extensive trade with peoples throughout the ancient world, spreading culinary traditions, resources, artisanal goods, and cultural norms to populations as disparate as the ancient peoples of Great Britain and the empires of China.

These routes depended on numerous skills and technologies to spread effectively, as well as on diplomacy and treaties. Early navigation technology made it possible for sea-adjacent communities to contact one another and establish relationships as early as the fourth millennia BCE. The development of better ships, including Phoenician models that were designed to withstand the rough waters of the Mediterranean, and more precise navigation technology made sea trade a fairly reliable source of goods and economic growth.

THE PHOENICIANS

Many large, great civilizations played a role in trade in the ancient world—but smaller populations also had an influential part to play. The Phoenicians were active from 1500 BCE to around 539 BCE and were based primarily in modern-day Syria and Lebanon. Merchants established a network of small trading ports in modern-day Tunisia, Cyprus, Greece, and Spain to facilitate their immense trade with other peoples. They spearheaded the sale of indigo dye, glass goods, and other luxury items from the Levant, which made them immensely wealthy despite their small size. Their shipbuilding and diplomacy skills ensured their longevity and power.

Land routes were also common in the ancient world, driven by the spread of domesticated animals like ox and camels. These routes were dotted with caravansarai. Land routes allowed Anatolia and the Caucasus—landlocked areas in modern-day Turkey and eastern Europe—to connect with civilizations in India, China, and the Middle East. Land routes from port areas, such as modern Spain or Greece, also played a role in spreading culture and information into landlocked areas. Diplomacy played an important role in maintaining trade routes; it was important for all areas through which merchants passed to ensure their protection against conflict, robbery, or other acts of violence that would disrupt the flow of goods and money.

PROJECT 3
CONNECTING EAST AND WEST

Research the Silk Road and create a map that shows the way the route spread, including information on what was traded at each major stopping point.

- Using the internet or your school library, research the Silk Road. Find information about the history of the Silk Road, including how it developed and when. What route did the Silk Road follow? Did the route change over time or stay mostly the same? What goods traveled along the Silk Road?

- Research the major stopping points along the Silk Road. These can include cities or smaller merchant towns. Why did a city or town develop as a stopping point for the Silk Road? What did these towns and cities offer merchants? What goods were traded at each point? What goods did merchants leave at these stops and what did they pick up to carry on their way?

- Using a template or drawing your own, create a map that shows the route of the Silk Road.
   o Include the starting point, major stops along the way, and the ending point. Be sure to include major cities or civilizations to show where the route was located in relation to other important places in the ancient world.
   o On your map, include a note about what goods were traded at each stopping point, indicating what was bought and what was sold. You can do so by using a color-coded key or by listing the items individually at each stop.

QUESTION 4 WHAT IMPACT DID THESE TRADE ROUTES HAVE ON THE ECONOMIES OF THE ANCIENT WORLD?

Trade drove culture forward, but it also shaped the economies of ancient civilizations. Trade routes were an important resource, bringing new currency and goods into cities and towns that could then be sold either to residents or other traders. Along with crucial staples, such as food, a market for luxury goods emerged quickly. Spices, textiles like silk, and glass goods became markers of significant wealth throughout the ancient world and in some cases marked royalty or other forms of elite society.

Trade was important for many reasons, including the fact that it provided much needed resources to places where food was scarce or goods were not easily accessed. But trade also made it possible for smaller states to flourish, such as Cyprus or Phoenicia, both of which were relatively small compared to greater empires but were nonetheless crucial to the trade routes that ran through them.

Similarly, trade gave rise to cities that went on to be historically significant, such as Carthage in modern-day Tunis, which began as a Phoenician outpost along the Mediterranean. Major cities can also track their history back to trade routes. The Silk Road alone drove the growth of cities like Kathmandu in Nepal, Kabul in Afghanistan, Tehran in Iran, and Aleppo in Syria. Trade cities would go on to be capitals and major hubs of growth, technology, knowledge, and culture for millennia— a testament to the importance trade played in shaping the ancient world.

PROJECT 4
THE CITIES THAT MADE TRADE POSSIBLE

Create a diorama of an ancient trade city, showing the ways in which trade fed the growth of major urban places that exist even today.

- Using the internet or your school library, research caravansarai or ancient trade cities. Choose one from near the middle of a trade route so that you can incorporate a mix of cultures and symbols.
- Find illustrations of what trade cities looked like, what kind of amenities they offered travelers, and how large they might have been. Pay close attention to the way architecture, food, clothing, and other cultural signifiers existed in these places.
- Using cardboard, paper, and other tools, create a diorama of a trade city. You can model it on one or more trade cities you have researched.
- Indicate roads, buildings, and other structures that show the way trade was part of the city's growth.
- Consider adding figures to show the many roles people in the community could carry out and how they related to trade. Also, show a variety of goods that would have passed through your trade city.
- You can include different phases of growth by showing some buildings that are under construction and making note of how trade allowed such places to flourish, either through incorporating materials that were traded in the city or by using cultural markings to show how knowledge and practices were exchanged along trade routes.

Create a diorama that shows how trade gave rise to cities, so that you and your class can understand why trade was so important in the ancient world.

- As part of your diorama, include a panel or poster with text explaining the way the city functioned, including specific information about the role of trade in encouraging business and growth. Also include the services offered to merchants and traders. Make sure to label your diorama to show important information that you explain in your poster.

COLONIZATION AND THE AGE OF EMPIRE

Empires have defined the history of the Eastern Hemisphere. Great empires such as the Greeks and Romans are considered the foundation of modern governance, while the Chinese and Persian empires gave rise to modern states that continue to play an important role in their regions and in world affairs. After

For most of history, empires such as the Roman Empire ruled large parts of the Eastern Hemisphere.

the fall of the Roman Empire around 476 CE, European empires like the Austro-Hungarian, Ottoman, and Russian empires began an ascent that would last until the twentieth century. Along with them came the rise of the British, French, Portuguese, and Dutch empires, which eventually controlled colonies around the Eastern Hemisphere until after World War II. These empires defined governance around the hemisphere for centuries and shaped relations between world powers, but in their aftermath countries around the world continue to struggle with the immense damage colonization had on local economies and cultures.

QUESTION 5 HOW DID EUROPEAN EMPIRES SPREAD AROUND THE WORLD?

The ancient world was dominated by large kingdoms and empires, which often conquered or lost nearby lands to rivals. The Romans were among the first to conquer significant parts of the entire Eastern ancient world, with holdings ranging across the hemisphere. After the fall of the Roman Empire in about 476 CE, Europe entered the Dark Ages, while in the Middle East and Asia empires continued to flourish, such as the Persians, the Chinese, the Indians, and the Ottomans. Together these empires held most of the Eastern Hemisphere, governing for centuries.

But that began to change in the 1300s and 1400s, when European powers began the Age of Exploration. The Dutch, Portuguese, French, and British were among the European powers that sent ships around the world, bringing Europeans in contact with cultures from which they had been isolated. They established colonies near ports, where they moved quickly to secure trade and resources—often at the expense of native populations.

By the beginning of the twentieth century, the British were the dominant world power, with colonies around the world. In fact, it was said that the sun never set on the British Empire, a reference to its presence in all parts of the globe. In the Eastern Hemisphere, the British controlled parts or all of Africa, Asia, India, and the Middle East. Practices by the British, as well as the French and Dutch, had a lasting impact on Africa, Asia, and other parts of the world. Colonization is linked predominantly to slowed economic growth, internal conflict due to efforts by colonizing powers to divide and conquer local populations, and difficulty establishing democratic forms of government. For much of the Eastern Hemisphere, the ramifications of the spread of empires remains among the chief concerns of the twenty-first century.

PROJECT 5
THE GROWTH OF EMPIRE

Create a timeline charting the spread over time of one European empire.

- Using the internet or your school library, research one European empire. You can choose the Dutch, Portuguese, British, French, or another. When did it begin sending expeditions to other parts of the world? What prompted it to begin? What route did its explorations take? This will likely include multiple expeditions to different parts of the world.
- Research where the country set up colonies in the Eastern Hemisphere. Some countries also established colonies in the Western Hemisphere, but those are not

to be included in the project. Why did the country set up colonies where it did? Was it because of resources, access to trade routes, or another reason? When were the colonies established? How much time elapsed between the establishment of colonies? When did the colony gain independence?

- Using a template or drawing your own, create a timeline that shows the spread of your selected empire. You can include other important dates, such as scientific breakthroughs, to provide context.

INDEPENDENCE MOVEMENTS

Colonialism was the reigning international norm for centuries—from around 1400 to the mid-1900s in various places around the world. But that doesn't mean that areas in which colonies were established didn't fight against foreign powers. In fact, independence movements were strong across Africa, Asia, the Middle East, and elsewhere; even in Europe, national identity often clashed with imperial powers. One movement that lasted for over a decade was the Mau Mau Uprising in Kenya. Although independence in Kenya was only gained in 1963, the Mau Mau Uprising began in 1952, bringing together numerous tribes to fight against British colonial rule. This was building on the work of earlier uprisings by groups like the Nandi Resistance of 1895 and the Giriama in 1913. The civil conflict with the Mau Mau was met with violent repression by the British, but eventually the Mau Mau succeeded in forcing Great Britain's hand in making Kenya an independent state.

QUESTION 6 WHAT ECONOMIC CONSIDERATIONS DROVE COLONIZATION?

Empires were established primarily for economic reasons, as control of resources and trade brought great wealth and power to European kingdoms. By gaining control of resources, empires were able to profit from the sale of items that were considered rare, such as metals or food goods. For example, the British were able to control the export of spices from India, a lucrative trade for private companies that gained control of those contracts and a resource the British were able to increase their own access to. This access, along with poorly paid or unpaid local labor, allowed wealth to flow into the countries at the heart of an empire.

Colonization was predicated on control of resources, but empires established their claims to those resources in differing ways. Particularly in the Eastern Hemisphere, colonizing powers often entered an area through private business, gaining a contract that assured them rights to a certain industry. The British East India Company held a monopoly on trade with and out of India from around 1600 to 1858, when the British Raj formalized Great Britain's control of the country. Similarly, in Persia (modern-day Iran), the British used contracts with the Qajar and Pahlavi dynasties to secure their sole right to economic resources and building, particularly after oil was discovered in the country in 1908. These methods differ sharply with other colonization models, many of which were based on more traditional means of warfare with local populations.

Colonization disrupted local economies in ways that are still being felt today. Colonizing powers often sought

Sea travel was key to the growth of colonial powers, allowing conquering powers to travel to the far reaches of the known world and bring back valuable resources.

to monopolize not only exports and imports, but the ways in which local populations were able to access their own resources. Through taxes, imposed shortages, or other means, colonizing powers overturned generations of tradition and created unstable systems. One example of this can be seen in Africa; in Kenya, the British imposed a food system that undermined the use of small kitchen gardens by making families walk miles and miles to purchase staple ingredients at overpriced markets. Elsewhere, colonizers controlled the most lucrative industries in any given colony, be it precious metals, foodstuff, or resources like oil.

PROJECT 6
COLONIZATION IN PRACTICE

Research differing models of colonization and create a presentation that compares and contrasts Britain's "spheres of influence" in Persia/Iran with colonial India.

- Using the internet or your school library, study how the British gained control of Persia (modern-day Iran) and India.

Create a presentation that shows the differing ways in which colonization took place, including through direct control and indirect control.

- What was the British East India Company? How did it create a defacto government within India?
- What led to the British East India Company being dissolved? What took its place?
- In Persia, how were "spheres of influence" enacted by the British and the Russian governments? What contracts were put in place to ensure Britain and Russia controlled most of the country?
- What was the Anglo-Persian Oil Company? How was it similar to the British East India Company? How was oil used to maintain British control of the country?
- Following the Russian Revolution, Russia gave up its claims in Persia. How did this change the governance of the country?
- Study the ways in which national movements pushed against colonial power. This can include protests against British power, leaders like Gandhi in India and Mossadegh in Iran, or ways in which governments tried to curtail foreign authority.
- Using an online tool or posterboard, create a presentation that explains the ways in which the British controlled Persia and India. Be sure to include the similarities and differences in how their control was established, the level of power they had in government, and any other details that show both how differently these two states were controlled and how similar the impact was on local populations.

CHAPTER FOUR

THE EARLY TWENTIETH CENTURY

In the first half of the twentieth century, the Eastern Hemisphere was shaken by wars, revolutions, and the collapse of empires that had ruled for centuries. World War I began in 1914, and by the time fighting stopped in 1918, Russia's monarchy had been unseated, the Ottoman Empire

During the twentieth century, war disrupted much of the Eastern Hemisphere and led to the development of new technology, cultural norms, and diplomatic initiatives.

was near collapse, and European powers were making plans to divide the Middle East into modern nation-states. In the late 1920s, a global depression hindered efforts to stabilize postwar Europe and fascism rose in Italy and Germany, while in Asia, Japan began pursuing an empire of its own. World War II broke out in 1935, and with this came the genocide of Jews and other marginalized people living under Nazi control. The conflict ended in 1945 but left behind a Europe ravaged by a decade of war, while the Soviet Union and China consolidated Communist control in the east. By 1950, the world looked very little like it did in 1900, and the aftermath of these seismic shifts is still felt today.

QUESTION 7 WHAT MADE THE WORLD WARS GLOBAL?

The World Wars drew almost every country on earth into conflict, but alliances were different during each war. World War I began in part due to the ways in which empires had aligned themselves through treaties and defense agreements, which created a domino effect when Austria declared war on Serbia in 1914. Countries like Germany and Great Britain had pledged support for their allies, which led to their declaring war in response. World War II, however, began in the aftermath of those empires' collapse, which created a massive change in how countries aligned themselves.

But those alliances are only one part of what created global war. Empires based in Europe, including the Ottomans and the British, controlled vast parts of the Eastern Hemisphere during World War I. During World War II, many colonies still existed in Africa, while in the Middle East, British and French power had been imposed in the aftermath of the Ottoman collapse. During both wars, colonial or imperial powers used local labor, soldiers, and resources to fuel the war effort, and fighting took place in areas that were formally neutral or controlled by outside powers.

PROJECT 7
A WORLD DIVIDED

Create a map that compares and contrasts alliances between World War I and World War II in the Eastern Hemisphere.

- Using the internet or your school library, research the alliances that were established during both World Wars in the Eastern Hemisphere.
    - o What was the status of colonial powers during both wars? How did this change between 1917 and 1935?
    - o How were colonies and countries in Africa and the Middle East involved in the wars?
    - o How were Asian countries allied during both of the wars?
    - o Which states remained neutral? Were they truly neutral, or did an outside power maintain a presence there, as the British did in Iran?
    - o Think about other ways in which power shifted hands between the wars and how that shaped alliances.
- Use a map template or draw your own. Create two maps to show how the alliances changed, color coding them to show what countries were fighting together.
    - o You can include a third color to show neutral states.
- You can also include indication of states that were colonized and therefore pulled into the conflict through the foreign power that controlled the area.

THE RUSSIAN REVOLUTION

Along with other European powers, Russia was a monarchy for much of its history. Ruled by a czar, Russia was one of the great centers of power in the early twentieth century, controlling large parts of Eurasia. But that changed in the later years of World War I. In 1917, Russia experienced not one but two revolutions. Growing inequality led to the violent overthrow of the government in early 1917, when people took to the streets of St. Petersburg to demand that Czar Nicholas II abolish the monarchy. A provisional government, which included far left parties, moderates, and former members of the czarist government, was established to rule over the vast Russian Empire. But the government struggled to work together, in part due to the agitation caused by the Bolsheviks, a group of Communists led by Vladimir Lenin. In October 1917, Lenin and his followers were able to seize power. This led to a civil war and the establishment of the Soviet Union, which would go on to become one of the most powerful governments in the world.

QUESTION 8 HOW DID COLONIAL POWER WEAKEN AFTER WORLD WAR II?

World War II left large parts of Europe in ruin, with economies across the Eastern Hemisphere struggling to recover after almost a decade of conflict. But the war also weakened colonial power around the world, much as World War I brought about the end of empires in many parts of the Eastern Hemisphere. The arguments underpinning World War II—namely that the Allies were fighting

The creation of the United Nations after World War II was a groundbreaking moment in the pursuit of human rights and peace between nations.

for universal human rights and democracy—were at odds with their treatment of colonies and non-European states, such as those in Africa and parts of Asia. After decades of seeing their work exploited and their resources used to power war rather than benefit the people in the colonies, nationalist leaders rose across Africa and Asia, challenging the authority of countries like Britain and France.

Independence movements had been active in colonized countries ever since colonial power was introduced, but norms and a lack of international law allowed foreign powers to use violence and force to oppress native populations. That began to change after World War II with the establishment of the United Nations, the Geneva Conventions, and other legal entities that sought to defend human rights. Although it would take decades in many cases, national movements gained steam in the years after World War II, and major blows to the authority of colonial powers made it difficult for them to justify maintaining a presence in former colonies.

This is not to say that states were left to their own devices following independence. Hegemony takes many forms, and as the age of colonies gave way to the Cold War, political alliances were often used to control countries while they maintained their own sovereignty. Powerful states, including those that were once colonial powers, are still able to exert more influence over smaller states, such as former colonies, through trade agreements, military cooperation, and cultural exchange. But the postcolonial world is one in which those exchanges continue to be questioned as we move toward a more equitable division of international power and influence.

PROJECT 8
EMPIRE IN CRISIS

Research the Suez Crisis in Egypt and create a presentation that explains how this crisis challenged British authority in Egypt and other colonial states.

- Using the internet or your school library, research the Suez Crisis of 1956.
  - o What is the Suez Canal? What role did it play in British power in the Middle East and North Africa?

The Suez Canal in Egypt was a center and symbol of colonial rule. But in the 1950s, it became the battleground in the Egyptian fight for independence.

o Who was Gamal Abdel Nasser? What was his platform in Egypt?

o What did the Suez Canal represent in Egyptian politics? Why was nationalizing it important?

o How did the crisis unfold? What role did Israel and France play in justifying British forces going into Egypt?

o What role did the United States play in the Suez Crisis? What does this suggest about the changing role of the United States in the post–World War II world?

- o How was the crisis resolved? Use primary sources to find out how leaders in all involved countries, particularly Egypt and Britain, framed the conflict for domestic audiences.
- Using an online tool such as Google Slides, create a presentation that explains what took place during the Suez Crisis. Include a discussion of the timeline of events, the politics of Egypt at that time, and why this crisis is seen as a turning point in world politics.
- Ask your classmates to respond to your presentation. You can ask them questions such as: Can you think of a parallel of the Suez Crisis either historically or today? How involved do you think nations should become in the affairs of other nations? Do you agree with the role Britain and/or the United States played in this crisis? Why or why not?

CHAPTER FIVE

THE COLD WAR

In the second half of the twentieth century, the Cold War between the Soviet Union (known as the USSR) and the United States defined world relations. A cold war is one in which no direct conflict takes place, but the tension between the two world powers and their rush to gain an upper hand over one other led to conflicts in Asia, the Middle East, and Africa. States were forced to align themselves with one of the two power poles of the era, creating tension within regions and

In the mid-twentieth century, the Soviet Union governed large parts of Eastern Europe as Communist states, creating conflict with the capitalist countries of Western Europe.

alienating leaders from their people. This gave rise to nationalist and independence movements in Africa and the Middle East, where a new era of leadership rose out of colonialism and cultural hegemony.

CHINA: COMMUNISM AND POWER

In the mid-twentieth century, conflict between capitalism and Communism defined world affairs. Communism, a philosophy based on sharing wealth that became popular in the late nineteenth and early twentieth centuries due to the work of Karl Marx, provided an economic and political blueprint for the Soviet Union. During the Cold War, the Soviet Union and the United States were the two poles of power, and the fall of the Soviet Union in the 1990s was seen as the end of the Communist era. But just south of eastern Russia, another Communist power, China, has become one of the world's most powerful nations. In 1931, the USSR helped launch a Communist uprising in China, led by Mao Zedong. The Chinese Communist Party fought against the Chinese government until 1949, when Mao's followers established the People's Republic of China. Mao ruled China until 1976, leading an era defined by unrest, famine, and suffering due to policies like the Cultural Revolution. Following his death, the Chinese government took steps to open the country up to international trade, but censorship and repression have remained significant issues inside the country, which is still ruled by the Communist Party.

QUESTION 9 HOW DID THE COLD WAR DIVIDE EUROPE?

After World War II, the Cold War between the United States and the Soviet Union shaped international politics while pushing the world dangerously close to a global nuclear war. Although they never actually directly fought, the two countries became poles of power around which the rest of the world—particularly the Eastern Hemisphere—arranged itself through alliances.

The Cold War created a stark division between European states, which continues to impact the economics and relations of the continent. Germany and its capital Berlin were divided by the Allied powers after World War II, creating a small microcosm of the tension seen on a continent-wide level. The Soviet Union quickly expanded to control the states in the former Russian Empire, which included much of the Caucasus and eastern Europe. Winston Churchill coined the term "Iron Curtain" to explain the clear line between Soviet and non-Soviet states. Belgium, France, Germany, Italy, Luxembourg, and the Netherlands started the European Economic Community (EEC), which would later become the European Union (EU). Soon after, in 1957, Denmark, Ireland, and the United Kingdom joined, establishing the EEC as an economic union, but it quickly became a counter to the Soviet Union. The United States established the North Atlantic Treaty Organization (NATO) to provide military cooperation as a bulwark against Soviet power.

Today the divisions created by this Cold War rivalry are stark. Many states that lived under Soviet Communist rule struggled with economic hardship, nondemocratic governments, and civil unrest, especially in the years following the fall of the Soviet Union in 1991. Some, like Ukraine, continue to struggle with Russian efforts to gain influence, while others are working to build a better future in the wake of dictatorship, suffering, and conflict.

PROJECT 9
EUROPE VERSUS EURASIA

Research the Iron Curtain and create a map that shows the divisions between European states during the Cold War.

- Using the internet or your school library, research the divisions within Europe during the Cold War.
  - o What did Winston Churchill mean when he referred to an "Iron Curtain" in Europe? How did this phrase describe the political situation in Europe during the Cold War?
  - o What countries fell under Soviet control, and which states remained outside of the Soviet Union?
  - o What was life like for those who lived on either side of the Iron Curtain? How were the politics of these countries different?
  - o How did the inequalities and differences between these states manifest after the fall of the Soviet Union? Which states have joined the European Union, and what can that tell us about the post–Soviet politics of Europe?
- Use a template or draw your own map, showing the Iron Curtain and which states fell on either side of it. You can include color coding to show what took place in each state after the fall of the Soviet Union.

QUESTION 10 WHAT IMPACT DID THE COLD WAR HAVE ON NON-EUROPEAN STATES?

The Cold War divided Europe in ways that are still being overcome today. But the Cold War also had an important impact on non-European countries, particularly those in Africa and Asia. The ideological divides that emerged during the Cold War—namely in regard to the economic policies of Communism and capitalism—became political divides as countries chose how to align themselves. Although the West's and the United States's allies used their economic and cultural influence to pressure states, choosing to align with the Soviet Union could also pose threats, especially as the United States moved to stop the spread of Communism.

The international community became pawns in the Cold War, as proxy conflicts emerged in places like Vietnam and Afghanistan. In these conflicts, the Soviet Union and the United States—with their allies—funded warring factions, creating a situation in which the two countries fought indirectly. Proxy warfare undermined local governance and created a dangerous precedent, in which genuine independence or reform movements could be framed as a threat to the United States or USSR to justify ongoing repression.

The tensions of the Cold War gave rise to a countermovement, with countries choosing to remain outside of the binary of power that the United States and USSR established. These countries sought independence from cultural or political influence, banding together in the Non-Aligned Movement. Still active today, the movement continues a conversation that began during the Cold War about how to maintain distance from superpowers.

Proxy wars between the Soviet Union and the United States had a significant and damaging impact on many Eastern Hemisphere nations, particularly in Asia and Africa.

PROJECT 10

NEITHER EAST NOR WEST

Research the Non-Aligned Movement and create a presentation on what it meant to remain unaligned with the dominant powers of the period.

- **Using the internet or your school library, research the Non-Aligned Movement.**

- When was the group started and why? Who were the founding members?
- What was the mission of the group when it was started?
- What countries have joined since it was established? What prompted them to do so?
- How did the mission of the group change after the fall of the Soviet Union? How does the group frame its mission and goals in the modern era?
- What are some critiques of the group? How has the international community responded? Has it been successful in its original or updated mission?
- Using an online tool, create a presentation that includes a timeline of the group, the states that have joined, work it carries out, and how it has achieved its goals.
- Be sure to include any leading critiques of the group and discussion of how it fit in the international community during the Cold War versus how it fits today.

QUESTION 11 HOW DID POLITICAL AND ECONOMIC IDEOLOGY INFLUENCE INTERNATIONAL RELATIONS DURING THE COLD WAR?

Economic ideology was at the heart of the conflict in the Cold War, and understanding the ways in which those ideologies clashed is key to understanding this prolonged period of history. The Soviet Union adhered to a repressive form of Communism, institutionalized first by Lenin through the violent repression of his opponents and then by his successor, Joseph Stalin, who ruled the Soviet Union with secrecy and violence. The economic system that underpinned the ideology of the Soviet Union was a state-planned form of extreme Communism, and the economy struggled to innovate at the rate of the West. But after the fall of the Soviet Union, many who had lived under the Communist system felt abandoned by a system that had provided basics like employment and housing for many.

The West, particularly the United States, adhered to a capitalist system. In the United States this meant laissez-faire economics and a free market, supplemented at times with a social safety net with programs like the New Deal. In the postwar boom of the 1950s, the United States was at the cutting edge of manufacturing and innovation, which in turn created a strong middle class—something the Soviet Union was unable to achieve. But the United States also struggled with repression; movements like the civil rights movement drove home the fact that economic freedom had to be paired with political freedom to be truly meaningful.

Even today experts and citizens debate the benefits and drawbacks of both capitalism and Communism, while many states have worked to take the best of both ideologies by introducing strong safety nets along with business-friendly economic policies. But the oppression instituted by the Soviet Union and the inconsistencies of the United States continue to throw doubt on how economic ideologies can be reconciled with political realities.

PROJECT 11
IDEOLOGIES AT WAR

Create a presentation that shows the differences between capitalism and Communism.

- Using the internet or your school library, research capitalism and Communism.
  - o What are the central ideas that make up each system? Who first introduced these ideas?
  - o What are the critiques of each system?
  - o How have these systems been put into practice? Have they fallen short of the original goals of each or have those goals been achieved?
  - o What is the source of tension between the two ideologies?
  - o Where does each ideology stand today?
- Using an online tool, create a presentation that explores the history of capitalism and Communism: how these systems were put to practice in the United States and USSR respectively, how politics and economics interacted in both states, and how this influenced the way we think about both ideologies today.
- Include graphs that show economic growth in both the Soviet Union and the United States during the Cold War as a way to explore these economic policies. This is a complex issue that is still the source of significant debate. Keep this in mind and be sure to draw from a wide range of sources, thinkers, and perspectives to gain a complete understanding of this question.

CHAPTER SIX

A NEW MILLENNIUM

Today, the Eastern Hemisphere is grappling with issues that can be traced far into the region's complex history. Ongoing conflict has driven millions from their homes and created tension within states from the Middle East to the Caucasus to Europe. Climate change threatens environments in vulnerable places, creating extreme weather that threatens ecosystems. But the countries of this hemisphere are more connected than ever, thanks to technology, a truly global economy, and international organizations that bring entire continents

One of the most pressing issues facing the world is climate change, which could be devastating for nations within the Eastern Hemisphere.

together. The way the states of the Eastern Hemisphere tackle and respond to the crises and concerns rocking the region will help determine the future of the entire world.

CLIMATE CHANGE IN THE TWENTY-FIRST CENTURY

Of the many issues facing the international community in the twenty-first century, climate change is perhaps the most persistent and critical. The Eastern Hemisphere faces some of the most cataclysmic consequences of unchecked climate change, ranging from desertification to rising sea levels. In India alone, drought in some areas and extreme flooding in others has been seen, threatening water supplies, agricultural areas, and high density urban areas. Climate change in the Middle East, Asia, and Africa could exacerbate existing conflicts, food shortages, and other issues that have created high levels of displacement or unrest.

QUESTION 12 WHAT COUNTRIES ARE SHAPING THE GLOBAL ECONOMY IN THE TWENTY-FIRST CENTURY?

The twentieth century saw the rise of a global economy, but one in which economic power was primarily held by the West. The postwar boom of the United States made it a cultural and business capital of the world, while cities like London and Berlin followed close behind as financial and cultural hubs. In the new millennium, however, the West has been challenged for its top spot in the world economy.

The twenty-first century has been marked primarily by rising economies, which are changing the way the world conducts business. The growth of information technology and the financial sector, as well as the ease of communication and travel, have allowed formerly overlooked cities to make a name for themselves as centers of world business. Dubai and Doha in the Middle East, Hong Kong and Tokyo in Asia, Rio de Janeiro in South America, and Johannesburg in Africa, as well as other cities, have implemented policies intended to support growth of new industries.

The rise of these cities has changed the way business is done on a global level, challenging how the world has thought of countries that were once overlooked. It has made former powers rethink how trade should be conducted while also giving rise to a new middle and upper class, and along with it a new luxury market. As the century continues, the rise of these states will define the world economy in ways that could reshape practices in numerous industries and the way we think about global business.

PROJECT 12
A NEW GLOBAL ECONOMY

Research the phenomenon known as the Rise of the Rest in the Eastern Hemisphere and create a presentation that shows the growth of formerly overlooked economies.

- **Using the internet or your school library, research rising economies.**

Research the changes in the world economy that are being driven by Eastern Hemisphere states, and share that information with your classmates.

o   What is the Rise of the Rest? What makes these countries unique in the global economy?

o   Choose three countries and do more in-depth research. Look for information like gross domestic product (GDP), growth industries, increases in exports, or other factors in their economies. You can use resources like the World Bank or the United Nations to find this information.

o What industries are largest in these countries? Has the government put in place any policies to encourage business?

o How have these economies grown in the past two decades?

• Using an online tool such as Canva or drawing your own, create a diagram that shows the growth of these economies. You can create three separate graphs or one that uses color coding to show how the countries have grown in comparison to one another.

o Include information about GDP, economic history, milestone legislation, or other interesting facts on your graphic.

QUESTION 13 HOW HAS CONFLICT SHAPED THE EASTERN HEMISPHERE?

Conflict in the twenty-first century has been very different from conflict in the past, with many issues rising in the Eastern Hemisphere as a result of ongoing unrest. International terrorism and the rise of non-state actors has been one of the era's most defining characteristics, which has fueled conflict in the Middle East, Africa, and Asia. Although not new to the twenty-first century, terrorism has become a major international concern with the rise of groups like the Islamic State of Iraq and Syria (ISIS), which displaced large numbers of people while carrying out numerous attacks around the Eastern Hemisphere.

Civil war and ethnic cleansing in countries like Syria, Libya, and Myanmar have further fueled unrest and displaced millions. According to the UN Refugee Agency, around 22.5 million people are currently refugees, or individuals forced to cross at least one border as a result of threats to their safety. This has created a dangerous situation, in which countries in the Middle East, Asia, Africa, and Europe have had resources for refugees strained. Millions are living in subpar housing or camps, children do not have access to education, and thousands have died on dangerous routes across land and sea. Meanwhile, a rise of xenophobia in countries that have taken in refugees has created tension between those in need and those who might help them, while driving a rise in nationalism.

PROJECT 13
DISPLACED PEOPLE

Research the refugee crisis that began in 2015 and create a map showing the crisis's movement across the hemisphere, including quotes from survivors and refugees that show their varied experiences.

- Use the internet to research the refugee crisis. The United Nations High Commission on Refugees is one great source, along with sources like the Council on Foreign Relations or Amnesty International.
  - o How many people have been displaced during the twenty-first century, and how many had been displaced before the year 2000?
  - o What conflicts forced refugees to leave their homes? Are these conflicts ongoing or have they ended?

o What countries are taking the most refugees? What routes are refugees following to get to safer countries?

o How are refugees received when they arrive in other countries? Are they welcomed or have they suffered xenophobia? This will differ from country to country, so be careful to collect information about multiple countries.

• Gather firsthand accounts of the journeys refugees take. Make sure you find accounts from multiple routes, destination countries, and origin countries. Look for adults as well as children and teens.

• Use a template or draw your own map, showing the routes along which refugees travel. Include land and water routes, showing the origin points and destination points.

o Use quotes from the firsthand accounts to create a sense of what the journey looks like and the struggles refugees face before, during, and after their journey. You can include these on the map itself if the quotes are short or include a key with points on the map labeled.

GLOSSARY

BRITISH EAST INDIA COMPANY A private British company that held all trade rights in India from 1600 to 1858.

CAPITALISM An economic ideology based on a free market and private ownership of business.

CARAVANSARAI Small cities that emerged along a trade route, often catering to merchants or traders.

CITY-STATE A contained urban space that functions as a country, such as the Vatican.

CIVILIZATION A population or region marked by a particular culture, way of life, and form of government.

CLIMATE CHANGE The gradual alteration of the Earth's weather patterns and temperature due to increasing levels of carbon dioxide in the atmosphere.

COLONIZATION A process by which a foreign power takes control of a region, country, or area.

COMMUNISM An economic and social ideology based on collectivism and public ownership of production.

CUNEIFORM An ancient form of writing made up of wedge-shaped letters, developed in Mesopotamia.

DARK AGES The period after the collapse of Roman rule in Europe, following which most of the continent fell into a period of unrest, disease, and struggle lasting from 476 CE to the 900s CE.

EASTERN HEMISPHERE A geographic region marked by the prime meridian in the west and the antimeridian in the east.

EMPIRE A large group of states or territories controlled by a monarch.

HEMISPHERE A geographic region made up of one half of Earth, divided along the prime meridian and the antimeridian for the Eastern and Western Hemispheres or the equator for the Northern and Southern Hemispheres.

INDIAN SUBCONTINENT The landmass in south Asia that contains India, Pakistan, and Bangladesh.

MILLENNIUM One thousand years.

OCEANIA The island nations in the South Pacific.

OTTOMAN EMPIRE An empire centered on modern-day Turkey that controlled much of the modern Middle East at its height.

PERSIAN EMPIRE An empire centered in Persia, or modern-day Iran.

PRIME MERIDIAN Located in Greenwich, England, it marks 0 degrees longitude.

SILK ROAD An ancient trade route that stretched from China to the Mediterranean, serving as one of the primary trade routes of the ancient world.

SPICE ROUTE A sea route that connected India to Asia, Africa, and other destination countries.

WESTERN HEMISPHERE A geographic region marked by the antimeridian in the west and the prime meridian in the east.

XENOPHOBIA Fear of people from other cultures or places, which often manifests as discrimination or racism.

FOR MORE INFORMATION

African Union
PO Box 3243
Roosevelt Street
W21K19 Addis Ababa
Ethiopia
Website: https://www.au.int
Email: dic@africa-union.org
Twitter: @_AfricanUnion

The African Union is a continent-wide organization assisting cooperation and development among member states. All African states, except for Morocco, are members in the group, which meets regularly and issues statements from the continent as a whole.

Asia Society and Museum
725 Park Avenue
New York, NY 10021
(212) 288-6400
Website: https://asiasociety.org
Email: info@asiasociety.org
Facebook and Twitter: @AsiaSociety

This nonprofit think tank focuses on various Asian issues, including trade across Asia, as well as promoting understanding between the people and institutions of Asia and the United States.

Canadian Association of African Studies (CAAS)
439 Paterson Hall
1125 Colonel By Drive
Carleton University
Ottawa ON K1S 5B6
Canada
(613) 520-2600 x 2270
Website: http://caas-acea.org
Email: caasacea@carleton.ca
This research institute brings together scholars who study Africa,
    including the continent's history, politics, and culture. CAAS
    also published a scholarly journal, *The Canadian Journal of
    African Studies*.

Centre for Southeast Asia Research (CSEAR)
Vancouver Campus
Institute of Asian Research, C.K. Choi Building 251
1855 West Mall
Vancouver, BC V6T 1Z2
Canada
(604) 822-4688
Website: https://cisar.iar.ubc.ca
Email: cisar.iar@ubc.ca
Facebook: @ UBCSoutheastAsia
Twitter: @ubc_sea
This research institute focuses on the study of India and Southeast
    Asia, including the region's history, politics, and culture.

Council of the European Union
Rue de la Loi/Wetstraat, 175
B-1048 Bruxelles

Belgium

Website: https://www.consilium.europea.eu

Facebook: @EUCouncil

Twitter: EUCouncilPress

The Council of the European Union (EU) is an institution that brings together governments from each of its member states to adopt laws and coordinate policies.

Middle East Institute (MEI)

1319 18th Street NW

Washington, DC 20036

(202) 785-1141

Website: http://mei.edu

Email: information@mei.edu

Twitter: @MiddleEastInstit

This nonprofit organization is dedicated to researching and providing analysis of breaking news in the Middle East and surrounding countries. MEI publishes work on economics, politics, conflict, and other issues.

FOR FURTHER READING

Beckman, Rosina. *Colonial and Postcolonial Africa*. New York, NY: Britannica Educational Publishing, 2017.

Blumenthal, Todd. *Earth's Hemispheres*. New York, NY: Gareth Stevens Publishing, 2018.

Chandler, Julia. *Colonial and Postcolonial East and Southeast Asia*. New York, NY: Britannica Educational Publishing, 2017.

Ellis, Catherine. *Colonial and Postcolonial South Asia*. New York, NY: Britannica Educational Publishing, 2017.

Harrison, Kathryn. *Mongols on the Silk Road*. New York, NY: Rosen Publishing, 2017.

Maxim, Bailey. *The Colonial and Postcolonial Middle East*. New York, NY: Britannica Educational Publishing, 2017.

Milson. *National Geographic World Cultures and Geography: Eastern Hemisphere*. Chicago, IL: National Geographic Learning, 2017.

Pellow, Randall A. and William C. Bucher. *The Eastern Hemisphere*. Lansdale, PA: Penns Valley Publishers, 2014.

Roscoe, Kelly. *The Emergence of Modern Europe*. New York, NY: Britannica Educational Publishing, 2018.

Santillian, Beatriz. *Alexander the Great*. New York, NY: Rosen Publishing, 2018.

Trenton, Russell. *The Russian Revolution*. New York, NY: Britannica Educational Publishing, 2016.

Uhl, Xina. *The Decline of Ancient Mesopotamian Civilization*. New York, NY: Rosen Publishing, 2017.

BIBLIOGRAPHY

Bates, Robert H. *When Things Fell Apart*. New York, NY: Cambridge University Press, 2008.

Chaudhuri, K. N. *Trade and Civilisation in the Indian Ocean*. Cambridge, MA: Cambridge University Press, 1985.

Cooper, Frederick. *Africa in the World: Capitalism, Empire, Nation-State*. Cambridge, MA: Harvard University Press, 2014.

Curtin, Phillip D. *Cross-Cultural Trade in World History*. Cambridge, UK: Cambridge University Press, 1984.

Frankopan, Peter. *The Silk Roads: A New History of the World*. New York, NY: Knopf Doubleday, 2016.

Fromkin, David. *A Peace to End All Peace: The Fall of the Ottoman Empire and the Creation of the Modern Middle East*. New York, NY: Henry Holt and Co, 1989.

Gasiorowski, Mark, David Long, and Bernard Reich, eds. *The Government and Politics of the Middle East and North Africa*. Boulder, CO: Perseus, 2014.

Gates, Charles. *Ancient Cities*. New York, NY: Routledge, 2003.

Hansen, Valerie. *The Silk Road*. Oxford, UK: Oxford University Press, 2012.

James, Lawrence. *Raj: The Making and Unmaking of British India*. New York, NY: St. Martin's Griffin, 2000.

Mansfield, Peter. *A History of the Middle East*. New York, NY: Penguin, 2013.

McIntosh, Jane. *Ancient Mesopotamia: New Perspectives*. Santa Barbara, CA: ABC-CLIO, 2005.

INDEX

ABOUT THE AUTHOR

Bridey Heing is a writer and book critic based in Washington, DC. She holds degrees in political science and international affairs from DePaul University and Washington University in Saint Louis. Her areas of focus are comparative politics and Iranian politics. Her master's thesis explores the evolution of populist politics and democracy in Iran since 1900. She has written about Iranian affairs, women's rights, and art and politics for publications like the *Economist*, Hyperallergic, and the Establishment. She also writes about literature and film. She enjoys traveling, reading, and exploring the many museums of Washington, DC.

PHOTO CREDITS

Design and Layout: Nicole Russo-Duca; Editor and Photo Researcher: Elizabeth Schmermund